"House of Grace, House of Blood moves far beyond the personal narrative to create an experience that clearly identifies the blade edge that is so-called American history, and invites the reader to consider how exclusion and connection hone it."

—MIHKU PAUL, author of *20th Century PowWow Playland.*

"This account of the violence of ignorance and the heartbreak of broken trust is all too frequent—and all too frequently silenced, ignored, miswritten, or forgotten in our collective societal reckoning with the truth of our nation's founding. And yet what Low seeks in *House of Grace, House of Blood,* what we who are compelled to bear witness in our verse seek in the telling, in the remembering, is a way forward through healing. The facts speak for themselves. The poet speaks for the dead—and those yet living."

—ABIGAIL CHABITNOY, author of *In the Current Where Drowning Is Beautiful*

"House of Grace, House of Blood is a masterpiece of both documentary poetry and Indigenous storytelling. Denise Low's exploration of history, memory, genealogy, and identity acknowledges the complexity of her bloodlines and the possibility of healing. Throughout, her poems become 'portals for hearing pleas / and scriptures.'"

—CRAIG SANTOS PEREZ, author of *From Unincorporated Territory [åmot]*

"With documentary and lyric intensity, Low claims poetry itself as memorial in her extraordinary new book."

—HADARA BAR-NADAV, author of *The Animal Is Chemical*

"In meticulously documenting the massacre of ninety-six Moravian Christian Indians in 1782 in powerful, heartbreaking poetry, Low does a service to poetry and history, and also honors the Indigenous peoples of North America, who have survived against all odds."

—LUCILLE LANG DAY, co-editor of *Red Indian Road West:
Native American Poetry from California*

"Denise Low's *House of Grace, House of Blood* chronicles the epigenetic expression of generational trauma left by the massacre of ninety-six Lenape Christian relatives inside a church in 1782. However, these poems also suggest epigenetic expressions of ancestral healing and reconciliation with living within contradictions, a powerful Indigenous inheritance that will leave you dancing in joyous resistance."

—EDGAR GABRIEL SILEX, author of *Acts of Love*

"The versatile and talented Denise Low ventures into documentary poetry in *House of Grace, House of Blood* with astonishing results. Through personal reflection, memories, imagined stories, chants, and collages of primary texts, she pieces together the story of one of the most heinous crimes against Indigenous people in North America. For Low, there are more questions than answers. These poems cinch the connections between religious and nationalist fervor, racial capitalism, and Indigenous survivance."

—JOSEPH HARRINGTON, author of *Disapparitions*

HOUSE OF GRACE, HOUSE OF BLOOD

DENISE LOW

HOUSE OF GRACE, HOUSE OF BLOOD

Poems

THE UNIVERSITY OF
ARIZONA PRESS
TUCSON

The University of Arizona Press
www.uapress.arizona.edu

We respectfully acknowledge the University of Arizona is on the land and territories of Indigenous peoples. Today, Arizona is home to twenty-two federally recognized tribes, with Tucson being home to the O'odham and the Yaqui. Committed to diversity and inclusion, the University strives to build sustainable relationships with sovereign Native Nations and Indigenous communities through education offerings, partnerships, and community service.

ISBN-13: 978-0-8165-5358-7 (paperback)
ISBN-13: 978-0-8165-5359-4 (ebook)

Cover design by Leigh McDonald
Cover art: *On Lenape Land* by Susan Hoenig, 2024. All rights reserved.
Designed and typeset by Leigh McDonald in Adobe Jensen Pro 11/13 and Kokoda WF (display)

Publication of this book is made possible in part by the proceeds of a permanent endowment created with the assistance of a Challenge Grant from the National Endowment for the Humanities, a federal agency.

Library of Congress Cataloging-in-Publication Data
Names: Low, Denise, author.
Title: House of grace, house of blood : poems / Denise Low.
Other titles: Sun tracks ; v. 96.
Description: Tucson : University of Arizona Press, 2024. | Series: Sun tracks ; volume 96
Identifiers: LCCN 2023052660 (print) | LCCN 2023052661 (ebook) | ISBN 9780816553587 (paperback) | ISBN 9780816553594 (ebook)
Subjects: LCSH: Gnadenhutten Massacre, Gnadenhutten, Ohio, 1782—Poetry. | Delaware Indians—History—18th century—Poetry. | LCGFT: Poetry.
Classification: LCC PS3562.O877 H68 2024 (print) | LCC PS3562.O877 (ebook) | DDC 811/.54—dc23/eng/20231229
LC record available at https://lccn.loc.gov/2023052660
LC ebook record available at https://lccn.loc.gov/2023052661

Printed in the United States of America
♾ This paper meets the requirements of ANSI/NISO Z39.48-1992 (Permanence of Paper).

Dedicated to Tom, who has joined the ancestors,

and to all our families by blood, marriage, and spirit.

CONTENTS

Preface   *xiii*

I. SLAUGHTER OF INNOCENTS, OHIO, MARCH 7–8, 1782

House of Grace, House of Blood   5

Their Names: First Shots at Gnadenhutten, 1782   6

Weapon of Choice, the Gnadenhutten Massacre, 1782   7

Their Names: The Children   8

Their Names: Benjamin Holmes   10

They Fled into the Forest   11

On the Ohio River, 1790   12

A Mixed-Blood's Questions   13

II. (NOT) EXTINCTION HISTORY / NOT (EXTINCTION) HISTORY

The Perpetrators Vow Not to Talk   17

Genocide Mathematics   18

Night Terrors   19

Undocumented Stories   20

Blood Documentation   21

Big Miller the Indian Fighter: Conversation with a Timeline   22

Time Moving through Flesh   23

III. WITNESS

A River's Witness   27

A Delaware Catechism   28

Colonial Belief: Canaanites   29

Walking with My Delaware Grandfather   30

IV. THE LORD'S PRAYERS

Hymns in the Forest	35
Translation: Psalm 27, Verse 4	36
Songs / Psalms	37
Translations: Gnadenhutten	38
Spelling Book for the Town of Gnadenhutten, 1782	39

V. TRAILS

Glyphs on Trees	43
The Forest Trail to Safety	44
Geography Lesson: Trail to / from a Massacre	45
Geography Lesson: "High-ways"	46
Geography Lesson: Of Rivers and Mountains and Stars	47
Some Survive	48
Doll Dance	49
Dance	51

VI. TRAIL MARKER TREES

Trail Marker Tree: Wisconsin	55
Trail Marker Tree: My Husband's Family History	56
At Delaware Relatives' [Stolen] Village in Ohio	57
No Fairy Tale	58
Grape	59
Settler Erasure / Desuetude	60
Seeds	61

VII. UPSTREAM

Acknowledgement of Lenape Lands	65
Geography Lesson: Diaspora	66
More Than Place Names	67
Census Form: What Color I[ndian]?	68
Ohio: Footstones in a Family Cemetery	69
Trails of My Relatives: Ohio to Kansas	70
Mary Ann (Bair / Bear / Bare)	72
Descendancy	73

VIII. THE CONTINUOUSLY GIVING FOREST

Baptism of Moravian Indian Converts, Pennsylvania, 1757   77

The Forest: Roots   78

The Forest: Warnings   79

The Forest: Damage   80

"Ohio" Means "Continuously Giving River"   81

IX. FIRE TRAILS

Archaeological Report I: Fire   85

Archaeological Report II: Corrections   86

Fire Terror / Fire Erasure   87

Family Research: Three Brothers   88

Jane's Maze, Delaware "Half-Breed Tract"   90

X. OHIO: MEMORIALS

Gnadenhutten Memorial Dedication, 1872   93

Memorial: The Cost   94

Postcard: "The Monument, Gnadenhutten, Ohio"   95

Signage: "Burial Site of Indian Martyrs"   96

"The White Men Called Them to Return": A Transcription   97

"The White Men Called Them to Return": An Interrogation   99

A Gambler's Odds   100

Stomp Dance, Wyandotte County, Kansas   101

Acknowledgments   103
Notes   105
Sources   107
Illustrations   109

PREFACE

LENAPE PEOPLE, or Delawares, were among the first Indigenous Americans to encounter Europeans in the northeastern United States. From the 1500s to the 1700s, many countries vied for supremacy in this region. Spanish, Swedes, Dutch, and English all attempted settlements in New Jersey and New York. Lenapes traded with them all, fought, were enslaved and sent to the Caribbean, lived free, farmed, and survived until driven west to Pennsylvania and Ohio. By the 19th century, their diaspora continued to Indiana, Wisconsin, Canada, Missouri, Kansas, Texas, Oklahoma, and Idaho. At each removal, they resisted until overcome by warfare and disease. At each removal, some stayed behind. Through my maternal grandfather, our family has ties to Delaware refugees who lived in Ohio and Kansas, as well as holdouts who stayed in New Jersey.

The 1782 massacre of a hundred Christian Delawares, who had converted to the pacifist Moravian faith, was especially heinous in the annals of genocide. A western Pennsylvania militia assembled without sanction of the Continental Army and traveled surreptitiously into Delaware treaty lands to plunder. Some Lenapes who evaded this group eventually found refuge in Ohio villages upstream from the massacre. European settler relatives of my maternal grandmother lived in Pennsylvania exactly where perpetrators of the massacre mustered.

Two Lenape boys escaped and relayed accounts of the murders to Moravian ministers, who recorded the history at the time. A Munsee woman escaped with her baby and hid in the forest, and she left her account to descendants, who informed Smithsonian fieldworkers in 1913–1914. *House of Grace, House of Blood* is based on these accounts and also on my fragmentary family traditions and other surviving oral and written sources. All errors are my own.

This collection of archival poetry celebrates the continuity of Lenape peoples in three federally recognized U.S. nations, in Canadian nations, in state communities, and many other situations for descendants of this history. I acknowledge all the conflicted history of my homeland and my family, with the intention that clarity can lead to healing.

—*Denise Low*

HOUSE OF GRACE, HOUSE OF BLOOD

I

SLAUGHTER OF INNOCENTS, OHIO, MARCH 7–8, 1782

MASSACRE OF THE CHRISTIAN INDIANS.

"Of the number thus cruelly murdered by the backwoodsmen of the upper Ohio, between fifty and sixty were women and children — some of them innocent babes."

You recall the time when the Jesus Indians of the Delawares lived near the Americans and had confidence in their promises of friendship. And thought they were secure, yet the Americans murdered all the men, women, and children, even as they prayed to Jesus. . . . When they killed them, no American ever was punished, not one.

—TECUMSEH, A SHAWNEE LEADER

The abominable Murders committed by some of the frontier People on the poor Moravian Indians has given me infinite Pain and Vexation. The Dispensations of Providence in this World puzzles my weak Reason. I cannot comprehend why cruel Men should have been permitted thus to destroy their Fellow Creatures.

—BENJAMIN FRANKLIN

HOUSE OF GRACE, HOUSE OF BLOOD

These white ribs   are crossbeams.
Prayers are breezes   blowing through lungs.

Two nests   my knuckles and phalanges
center each grasp   each hunger.

Ears are portals   for hearing pleas
and scriptures—   words of possibilities.

Eyes are sentries   judging friend or not
and who   may be safe in this house.

This soft tongue   is sensor of flavors
singer of memories   an organ of thirst.

This heart   powers blood through flesh
also anger—   the fierce kindling of murder.

Scent of mother's milk   is the first miracle—
the body's red streams   turned white and sweet.

THEIR NAMES

First Shots at Gnadenhutten, 1782

A mile from town, the renegade militia spot a lone Indian walking, Joseph Shabosh.
  Lieutenant Colonel David Williamson was the highest-ranking officer

They fire shots at Shabosh, who falls to the ground with a broken arm.
  Joseph Vance, an elder in Cross Creek Church, led prayers for those planning murder

Assuming they are mistaking him for someone else, Shabosh does not flee.
  Captain Thomas Rankin was one of the most affluent men

Shabosh pleads that he is a local Christian Indian and the son of John Bull from England.
  Lieutenant John Carpenter, like many, had settled illegally on Indian [sic] lands

The whites seize young Shabosh and chop him to pieces with their tomahawks.
  Sam Hindman was one of the most violent

Joseph Shabosh cries out between blows and implores them to spare him.
  Charles Bilderback is the man who struck the final blow

Revolutionary War militia men were required to carry a "tomahawk" or "cutting sword."

English traders sell tomahawks
with a curved steel blade on one end,
a steel pipe bowl on the other.
  Nota bene: Tomahawk, Powhatan tamahaac,
  "temah," to cut off with a tool.
  First recorded, 1610.

Woodcutting is a daily task
for settlers and for Lenapes.
A hatchet / tomahawk is a daily tool.
  Nota bene: Middle English hachet,
  Anglo-French *hachette*, a small battle-ax.
  First known use, 14th century.

Note: Because I look "white,"
settler descendants tell me about "Indians"
and their scalp-taking tomahawks.
  Old German *akwisi*, Old English *axe*,
  American English ax: a weapon / cutting tool.
  First written use, 8th century.

Note well: my father's mixed-blood grandfather
would not "touch" tobacco. He prayed
with a Christian book, no pipe of tobacco.
  My Menominee husband gifts me
  a Lenape *təmahikan* / cut-off tool
  (tomahawk-pipe). We smoke and pray.

At Gnadenhutten *Nathan Rollins tomahawked*
19 Moravians. Militia scalped every child,
woman, and man. The bounty proclamation of 1780 reads:

  Order of Joseph Reed of Pennsylvania, a reward
  of two-thousand five-hundred continental dollars
  for every Indian Scalp.

Note: Dated two years before the Gnadenhutten murders.

THEIR NAMES

The Children

*

The Christian Delawares, starving in a prison camp,
returned to harvest their cornfield.

> *Among the children killed were: John Martin's sons*

Pittsburgh militia tracked them to Gnadenhutten.
Some were Paxton Boys. Others became Whiskey Rebels.

> *and Widow Mary's daughter Hannah*

The raiders hailed the Lenape laborers as their friends.
They would accompany them to Fort Pitt for safety, they said.

> *and Maria Elizabeth, daughter of Mark Delaware*

The raiders fell upon their bewildered prisoners.

> *and Gottlieb and Benjamin, Joanna's sons.*

The militia voted whether the Moravians should be burned alive or tomahawked and
scalped.

> *More killed were little Anthony and John Thomas*

One of the women who had been educated in Pennsylvania fell on her knees
at Williamson's feet and besought his protection.

> *and Christian, Joseph, Mark, Jonathan*

*

The raiders confined the men in a cooper's house
where they found a mallet. One said, "How exactly this will answer for the business!"

> *also Gottlieb and Timothy, Jonah, Christiana, Leah*

His name was Leet.

> *And Benigna, Gertrude, and thirteen babes not baptized*

In the house of women and children, the massacre began with Judith, an old and pious
widow.

> *More murdered children were Christina, Anna Christina,*
> *Anna, Salome, and Anna Elizabeth*

Many children were killed in their mothers' arms. All were scalped, many while still alive.

Anna, Bathsheba—daughters of Gnadenhutten's founder

Afterwards, the executioners gathered their trophies and plunder. They stole fifty horses.
Older girls killed were Anna, Salome, Anna Elizabeth

The raiders set fire to cabins and spent the night in drunken revelry by light of the burning shambles.

John, a youth, was shot swimming the river

THEIR NAMES

Benjamin Holmes

Obadiah Holmes
> one of (only) eighteen
> who refused to kill

brought home
> a Lenape boy
> Benjamin

who, in the confusion,
> ran to him.

> Obadiah Holmes later
> > broke his vow of silence:

> > *Nathan Rollins & his brother,*
> > *who had a father & uncle killed,*
> > *took the lead in murdering the Indians,*

> > *. . . & Nathan Rollins tomahawked*
> > *nineteen of the poor Moravians.*
> > *. . . & after it was over he sat down*

> > *& said it was no satisfaction*
> > *for the loss of his father & uncle*
> > *after all.*

Benjamin Holmes
> lived with Obadiah
> until grown.

He disappeared afterward
> from settler history.

> He enters these pages
> as a grown Lenape man:

> Benjamin Holmes.

THEY FLED INTO THE FOREST

Two boys escape the slaughter, Thomas and Jacob. Thomas, knocked down and scalped with the rest, feigns death. He crawls over the dead bodies and flees into the forest.

> *Thomas's scalp wound causes fits. He later will fall into the river during a fit and drown.*

Two boys escape, Thomas and Jacob. Jacob, having concealed himself beneath the women and children's cabin floorboards, remains hidden. Blood drips through the cracks all through the murders. After dark, he climbs out a window.

> *Jacob lies quietly all day as the murderers kill his mother and other children with a mallet and tomahawks. All day he lies unmoving in their blood.*

Thomas and Jacob flee along the Sandusky Trail. They warn another Moravian village and save them.

> *No longer are they children.*

Thomas and Jacob flee Gnadenhutten. They arrive at a mission where Moravian clergy write their story. No military report exists.

> *The killers know their guilt.*

Thomas and Jacob tell us this story.

ON THE OHIO RIVER, 1790

This day   two fathers
rise at sunbreak   and go to
the water   wade in its icy mud
shallows—   their faces mirror
reflections   on this day
they will fight   each other.

Downstream   moon faces
of two mothers reflect   in water
They both   carry babies.
Soon after drinking   dawn's
blood river   they will be widows.

A MIXED-BLOOD'S QUESTIONS

Which hand do I choose? So quick am I
to say the clean one. Not the bloody one
that prevailed. Only blameless martyrs
made my body, I say. Not brutes.

Which grandfather rides a wagon
on red-brick streets and never arrives?
Which grandmother sets aside sewing,
banks embers, and cannot sleep?

Both Lenapes and whites live in
wooden frame houses. Both fight
Southern slave holders. Both tend
apple orchards and homesteads.

They farm corn, beans, and squash—
plants alive in my flesh. Whose
bodies are untainted? What blood
passes to me only in acts of love?

II

—

(NOT) EXTINCTION HISTORY / NOT (EXTINCTION) HISTORY

Document Genocide (n. dok'hu ment' jen'e sid'), n. 1. The deliberate extermination of a race of people through changing information about them in an official paper.
—ROSE POWHATAN

THE PERPETRATORS VOW NOT TO TALK

The raiders gather Moravian goods for auction, scalps for bounties, and stolen horses. They set out from Gnadenhutten.

> *For the slaughter of Moravians, Daniel Leet was the first soldier who used the mallet. William Welch, an Irishman, killed seven with a tomahawk.*

They travel all night and reach Mingo on Saturday afternoon, where they halt long enough to retie the plunder on their horses. They cross the river.

> *Dave Slaughter swam the icy river to bring a wooden maple sugar trough so the men could transport their clothes dry, after they all swam the Muskingum River.*

They worry they might be called to account for the massacre by military authorities at Fort Pitt. They vow not to talk.

> *Solomon was the man who, years later, pantomimed scalping victims in the raid whenever he was drunk.*

No expedition of equal importance, military or civil, so suddenly and so entirely disappears from public notice.

> *An African slave noticed how, after the journey, his owner's horse was streaked with blood from fresh scalps. The owner spent the next day stretching scalps on frames and drying them by the fire.*

GENOCIDE MATHEMATICS

Story Problem:

"The Pennsylvania militia brought back
96 scalps."

[Who made this grisly count?
Were they laid out on display and totaled?]

"According to computation made by the missionaries,
the number of Delaware Christian victims was
90."

[They killed Christian converts and traditional Lenapes,
mutilated the bodies, and burned everyone
together.]

"6 of the murdered ones
must have been heathen [sic],
visitors at Gnadenhutten."

96-90 = 6

Conversion Tables: Value of a Life

In Continental dollars $2500
per bounty as decreed by the governor
= $33.33 sterling.
Sums: 96 scalps at $33.33 @ =
$3,199.68.

$1 in 1776 in purchasing power
is $34.58 in 2023.

Sums: Bounties for 96 people = $3,199.63 sterling in 1782
Sums: Bounties for 96 people= $110,643.21 in 2023

Sums: Bounty per person = $33.33 sterling in 1782
Sums: Bounty per person =

$1,152.53 in 2023

NIGHT TERRORS

I awaken and switch on a lamp.

My Lenape grandfather is already awake.

We listen to the dark.

Cicadas drone with the wind.

Tonight, nothing worse.

UNDOCUMENTED STORIES

*

A history lesson, I am four:
an old white man rides into town
looming on a horse-drawn wagon.
Hooves clatter on brick cobbles.

His wrinkled face is a museum,
a frontier relic. His parched cheeks
and creased fists grasping reins
show time's tracks in flesh.

*

A man living in Kansas tells this story:
> The village was by the Mississippi.
> When the killing ended, two toddlers
> cried under a cookpot. An army recruit
> did not bayonet the girls but instead
> defied guns trained at his back.
> He took them home to his wife.
> The soldier was his grandfather,
> the younger baby was his mother.

*

My Irish-and-German grandmothers
recount worries of the world wars.
They describe no rubber, no steel.
One leaves diamonds, the other lace.

*

My Christian grandfather urges
me to rise early in the morning,
"Atone. Say your prayers.
Forget our Indian past. It is over."

The brown-skinned grandfather stares
at me from the mirror at daybreak.
I cannot escape his eyes. We know
the continuing grief of Gnadenhutten.

BLOOD DOCUMENTATION

I read the list of Gnadenhutten victims with dread.
I read the list of Pennsylvania militia with dread.

Is Big Miller, my several-great grandfather, one of them?
Is he the officer commissioned for the massacre?
Are my relatives Wallace and Ross with him?

Is the Gnadenhutten crime within my bloodline
as well as the fate of nameless ones who were killed,
their names lost even to the Delaware nations?

BIG MILLER THE INDIAN FIGHTER

Conversation with a Timeline

1780 My second-great grandfather William,
his brother John, and mother Hanna Ross "settle"
in Washington County to escape "Indian problems"
   Did you understand you were colonizer problems?

1782 Cornelius serves under his uncle Henry Enoch
during the Revolutionary War, Washington County militia.
   Did you also serve under David Williamson—
   the leader at Gnadenhutten?

1782 the Fourth Battalion of the militia rides
to Gnadenhutten, with William and Robert Miller.
   Are you this William Miller? Is Robert Miller my uncle?

1783 After Gnadenhutten, he travels the Ohio River to Fort Washington.
He takes employment as an Indian scout.
   Did you understand you were an invader?

1790 Cornelius, while going for supplies,
is captured, killed, and scalped.
   Did you know your enemies?

1790 Com is the Delaware man who killed him.
   Was he also my relative?

The obituary of William Cornelius Miller's grandson gives this story:
   As Indians attacked the fort they bragged and shouted,
   "Big Miller is killed, we got Big Miller."

TIME MOVING THROUGH FLESH

As my grandfather
held me

I hold this baby
see what she sees

in old eyes like
Grandfather's.

She knows
her future through

hazel portals
also looks back

to Gnadenhutten,
those murders.

We rest in this
moment. No crows

disrupt trees.
Light rain falls.

III

—

WITNESS

During their labors their daily meetings were kept under the broad canopy of heaven. When the shadows of evening fell upon them, they seated themselves around fires in the open air; one of the missionaries delivering to the listening circle a short discourse. At times, some of the strolling savages would also attend, not to hear the gospel preached, but to scoff and laugh.

—TRUE HISTORY OF THE MASSACRE OF NINETY-SIX CHRISTIAN INDIANS

A RIVER'S WITNESS

*

Lenape traders travel the Muskingum in dugouts
        purveying salt, furs, shells, and pearls.

For centuries their wooden barges carry full cargoes.
        Hunters and fighters use quick birchbark canoes.

*

A Delaware elder tells me how missionaries taught writing,
        how paper treaties stayed safe in a wooden chest.

During removal west, at a river crossing, the boat
        capsized. The waters took all Lenape records.

*

By the Little Muskingum, muddy brown as an elk's eye,
        the current swallows voices of both killers and victims.

Their echoes drown in the snowmelt torrent
        as the river's thunder rises to heaven.

*

Ink washes into winter's flow and also blood—
        traces never completely dissolved. Even now,

as mussels pearl themselves colors of dawn glimmering
        on the river, all passings entangle at once.

A DELAWARE CATECHISM

"The Delaware believe in survival
of the spirit after death."

> Traditional Delawares believe in dreams
> in spirit moving within all people
> in sacred breath of speech.

"The spirit leaves earth to go
to another place where
it can be free from
miseries of this world."

> Spirit exists in plants and animals
> in rocks, soil, mountains,
> waters, winds, sun, moon.

"The Delawares believe
the spirit leaves earth to journey
to the stars."

> They believe in life beyond miseries
> beyond twelve layers of heavens
> beyond the grief of Gnadenhutten.

COLONIAL BELIEF

Canaanites

At a poetry reading a woman from Georgia rises
and says as a Black woman and Lesbian,
she is rewriting the bible,
to purge it of slavery and genocide.

> *"But thou shalt utterly destroy them;*
> *namely, the Hittites, and the Amorites,*
> *the Canaanites, and the Perizzites . . .*
> *as the Lord thy God hath commanded thee."*
> *Deuteronomy 20:17.*

After the poetry reading I offer the woman
my Canaanite grandfather's hand
and also the other grandfather's,
the one that killed Canaanites.
She clasps both.

> *"They professed to believe that the Indians*
> *were Canaanites of the western world,*
> *that God's command to Joshua to destroy*
> *held good with regards to the American Indians."*

WALKING WITH MY DELAWARE GRANDFATHER

Walking home I feel a presence following
        and realize he is always there

that Native man with coal-black-hair who is
        my grandfather. In my first memories

he is present, mostly wordless,
        resident in the house where I was born.

My mother shows him the cleft in my chin
        identical to his. I am swaddled

and blinking in the kitchen light. So
        we are introduced. We never part.

Sometimes I forget he lodges in my house still,
        the bone-house where my heart beats.

I carry his mother's framework
        a sturdy structure. I learn his birthright.

I hear his mother's teachings through
        what my mother said of her:

She kept a pot of stew on the stove
        all day for anyone to eat.

She never went to church but said
        you could be a good person anyway.

She fed hoboes during the '30s,
        her back porch a regular stopover.

Every person has rights no matter
        what color. Be respectful.

This son of hers, my grandfather,
        still walks the streets with me.

Some twist of blood and heat still spark
        across the time bridge. Here, listen:

Air draws through these lungs made from his.
        His blood still pulses through this hand.

IV

—

THE LORD'S PRAYERS

Ki Vetochemelenk, talli epian Awossagame. Machelendosutsch Ktellewunsowoagan Ksakimowagan peyewiketsch Ktelitehewagan leketsch yun Achquidhackanike elgiqui leek talli Awossagame Milineen eligischquik qunagischuk Achpoan woak miwelendammauwineen n'tschannauchsowagan nena elgiqui niluna miwelendammauwenk nik tschetschanilawequengik woak kalschi n'pawuneen li chquelschlowaganink shuckund ktennineen untschi medhicking Alod Knihillatamen ksakimowagan woak ktallewussoagan woak ktallowilissowagan ne untschi nallemiwi Nanne leketsch.

—MUNSEE LANGUAGE

Thou our Father there dwelling beyond the clouds, magnified thy name; thy kingdom come on; thy thought come to pass here all over the earth. The same as it is there beyond the clouds. Through this day the usual daily bread, and forgive to us our transgressions, the same as we who are here we mutually forgive them who have injured us, and let us come to that, that we fall into temptation, rather keep us free from all evil, for thou claimest kingdom and the superior power and all magnificence from heretofore always, amen.

—LITERAL TRANSLATION FROM MUNSEE

Our father which art in heaven, hallowed be thy Name. Thy kingdom come, thy will be done in Earth as it is in heaven. Give us this day our daily bread and forgive us our debts as we forgive our debtors. Lead us not into temptation but deliver us from evil, for thine is the kingdom and the power and the glory forever. Amen.

—KING JAMES BIBLE

HYMNS IN THE FOREST

Moravian Christians loved lutes,
brass fanfares, wooden double flutes,
and biblical texts as hymns.

> *"During organization of Bethlehem*
> *in Pennsylvania, strolling groups*
> *of Indians were visitors."*

Moravians prayed with melodies,
with mandolins and violins,
with choruses of loud oboes.

> *"Some were escorted to the Chapel*
> *where Moravians entertained them*
> *with instrumental music."*

Moravians sang their devotions.
They plucked, fiddled, and trilled arias,
filling the forest with tunes.

> Sweet as honey the music promised
> chords in perfect order
> in Heaven above, in the stars.

But on Earth, harmony lasts only
as long as the bass solo drone circles
trees the night before a massacre.

TRANSLATION

Psalm 27, Verse 4

"That I may dwell
in the house of the Lord
all the days of my life,

       That I may dwell in the house
       of grace all the days of my life
       and enquire in his temple,

to behold the beauty
of the Lord, and to enquire
in his temple."

       to behold the grace beyond
       Gnadenhutten's blood
       to behold beauty in the Earth,

       and find grace in the North,
       in the West, in the South,
       and new beginnings of the East.

SONGS / PSALMS

Delaware women know Doll Dance songs
  and water maps of the coastline.
Women carry seeds:
   Shackamoxen beans, blue Sehapsing corn.
They weave baskets with stories plaited into weft:
   water designs and sun's path.
Their cradle boards carry babies who will learn.

Men know bear hunting songs,
  protection songs, herbs for war.
They know maps of the Milky Way,
   family hunting territories,
   the trails along the Great Lakes.
They know how to dream and pray.
   They know how to say *wanishi*.

TRANSLATIONS

Gnadenhutten

Gnadenhutten
House of grace

Gnadenhutten
Place of graced deaths

Gnadenhutten
Tabernacle of grace

Gnadenhutten
Wooden hut graced by prayer

Gnadenhutten
Blood graced by psalms

Gnadenhutten
Bloodied house

Gnadenhutten
Graced rafters burned

Gnadenhutten
Ashes of grace

SPELLING BOOK FOR THE TOWN OF GNADENHUTTEN, 1782

A Delaware Indian and English Spelling-Book
for the Use of the Schools of the Christian Indians
on Muskingum River by David Zeisberger, Missionary:

Letters recited—A, B, C—
Bible stories sounded,
prayers memorized,

vowels on lips voiced
in New Testament verses,
"Love thine enemies."

They learn cursive script
until one day the killers
erase all lessons.

In the burnt schoolroom
pages turn to ashes
settling on the forest floor.

No one learns silent
"-gh" in "might" and "right"
and "g" in "foreign."

No one repeats Gospel
verses on cold afternoons
of Ohio winters.

What spelled-out words
on lips can un-spell
the spell of Gnadenhutten?

ESSAY

OF A

Delaware-Indian and *English*

SPELLING-BOOK,

FOR THE

USE OF THE SCHOOLS

OF THE

CHRISTIAN INDIANS
on *Muskingum River*.

By DAVID ZEISBERGER,
MISSIONARY among the *Western Indians*.

PHILADELPHIA,
Printed by HENRY MILLER. 1776.

V

—

TRAILS

The Village of Gnadenhutten

The stone foundations of the cabins, some aged apple-trees planted by their hands, and a few pathetic traces of the fire that consumed the victims of the massacre alone remain to attest the success and the disastrous close of the Moravians' loving and devoted labors at Gnadenhütten.

—WILLIAM DEAN HOWELLS

GLYPHS ON TREES

Delaware hieroglyphics were characteristic figures which were frequently painted upon trees. . . .
They generally preferred a tall, well-grown tree; they then would peel the bark on one side,
scrape the wood till it became white and clean, then draw the figure.
                                              —WILLIAM HELLER

What glyph for the woman and her baby fleeing Gnadenhutten?
     : 3 overnight campfire rings
     or
     : 1 figure of a woman not killed

What glyph for the Lenape hunters who escaped?
     : "the right path" glyph to hunting territories
     or
     : the single trail to safety

What glyph to choose for Gnadenhutten?
     : a church in flames
     or
     : 96 corpses / crosses

What glyph to choose for heroes of Gnadenhutten?
     : 2 figures of the boys who escaped to warn others
     or
     : figures of 96 people on 96 separate trees
          each tree a monument

What glyphs last beyond fifty years?
     : lightning-struck figures fading on wood
     or
     : these twisted sticks of letters

THE FOREST TRAIL TO SAFETY

Thomas and Jacob escape to the forest,
a place of game trails and portages,
sugar maples and hickory groves,
wild ginseng and willow bark medicine,
riverbanks and catfish washouts,

marshes between bluffs with wild rice,
birches bent to show directions—
footpaths along the Little Muskingum,
winter camp sites on the Scioto Trail,
Cuyahoga War Trail, the Tuscarawas.

They flee past strawberry meadows
and an oak tree struck by lightning,
past creekside blackberry thickets,
red foxtail squirrels chattering alarms,
past rock overhang shelters with hearths

and boulders etched with turtles and men,
around mounds of sacred burials,
through fields of corn, beans, and squash.
Jacob, Thomas, and Schoenbrunn villagers
escape, safe from the flames of Gnadenhutten.

GEOGRAPHY LESSON

Trail to / from a Massacre

Western Pennsylvania, Washington County,
Wissameking (Catfish Camp), is the starting point
of the war journey: Destined killers saddle horses
and pack. They hail from Scotland and Ireland.

They believe Indians are Canaanites without souls.
First stop, over mountains and down, is Cross Creek.
They follow rivers through West Virginia's panhandle
to Ohio. Some soldiers walk. They are two-hundred

men strong. Wheeling, next stop, is *Wih link*, "Place
of the Head." A settler's decapitated head once hung
at the Wheeling Creek confluence. Horses and men
swim chilled snowmelt water. Night brings frost.

Past the Ohio, the path cuts north to the Muskingum.
They stop at last near Gnadenhutten and camp quietly.
Perhaps they pray this last night before the slaughter.
They are men a while longer. Some mourn wives.

Some seized Delaware land and want to keep it.
Some hate "Indians." Some drink whiskey and doze
this last night of venal grace and dreamless sleep
before they murder a pacifist Christian people.

GEOGRAPHY LESSON

"High-ways"

The trail to Gnadenhutten leads through dense forests crossed by rivers and streams.

"Original traces through the dense forest of Ohio were created by animals such as buffalo and deer in search of food, water, and salt licks."

The way to Gnadenhutten follows a game trail from Lenapehoking to Ohio.

"Trails were far enough from streams to avoid swamps and sometimes followed the ridges and became known as "high-ways."

The single-file trail to Gnadenhutten leads to a flint quarry.

"Efficient travel was on streams, rivers, and lakes by canoe."

Travelers must portage upstream through shallows.

"Paths were narrow, well-worn, and difficult to travel."

Across a great distance and across centuries, those on the Ohio high-ways travel and carry stories.

GEOGRAPHY LESSON

Of Rivers and Mountains and Stars

Delawares never are lost in a forest.

*

By night they follow the North Star,
by day, glyphs etched on tree bark.
They find places exactly.

They mark longer distances
by a day's walking time
counting fifteen or twenty miles each.

These they divide into half-days.
They know exactly the distance
for hunting journeys and for war.

*

Lectio divina, I read sky's text thrice,
feel what West-wind shift to North
touches my cheek and what sleet

greets the winter's sunken sun,
what feelings rise from the body,
what memory lodges in my heart.

My ears can listen for clink
of metal and can hear voices
calling me away from danger.

SOME SURVIVE

The Lenapes not killed:
       Jacob, who watches from behind a tree
       A boy who hides under bloody floorboards, also named Jacob
       One who feigns death in a heap of bodies, named Thomas
       A small boy Benjamin, saved by Obadiah Holmes
       A woman and her baby hidden in trees beside the road
       Shabosh's second son, away when the militia arrives
       Those in a nearby village, warned by Jacob and Thomas.

Refugees flee Gnadenhutten:
       to Apple Creek, where my grandparents will live
       to Sugar Creek, where other grandparents will live
       to Captive Town on the Sandusky River

       north to Canada
       east, back to Lenapehoking
       west into the forests
       southwest into the grasslands

Delawares alive today—enrolled or not, adopted, orphaned, hidden—
       we all survive genocide.

DOLL DANCE

During the long middle years of wandering, the four-plus decades in Missouri and Kansas,
Grandma . . . became keeper of the Ohtas, the Delaware dolls.
—LYNETTE PERRY

*

In the story a Lenape girl played
      alone by an oak and made a doll.
When she added eyes and a mouth
      it said, "Keep me. I can help you,"

but the girl left it behind. That night
      in her dreams it kept crying,
"Where are you?" Other orphans
        wander lost in forests:

Hansel and Gretel were abandoned
      and found a witch's cottage.
Hero Twins of the Mayans were beheaded
      in Underworld jungles.

The girl may have played with husks
      of the sacred corn before
she made the doll, what her grandmother
      told her never to do.

*

The Doll spent a night of no moon
      naked under frost-covered leaves.
At dawn the Lenape girl ran back
      and found it shivering and alive.

What happened all that long night
      of endless waiting, of grief
so bad it traveled to the dream world?
      But the story is lucky. The Doll was found.

The Doll said, "Keep me, and your family
      will always be happy and healthy.
Every spring, you will sew me a new dress
      and hold a feast for me."

The girl made a red wraparound skirt
        trimmed in black to honor winter.
She listened to the Doll and learned
        its dance, its song, its love of corn.

*

My great-grandmother dressed her dolls
        and honored them each year
even though she never learned the Doll Dance
        in Christian Ohio. She had no Ohtas

but knew of healing from such dolls,
        not baby dolls but guardians.
She dressed her own daughters in red finery
        because the world would depend on them.

Grandmother taught my mother to sew clothes
        from her children's leftover fabric.
She sewed new finery for the family's dolls—
        skirts for the women, vests for the men.

Each Christmas my mother made me gifts—
        hand-sewn doll blouses, gathered skirts.
Each year I hid disappointment until
        my dressed dolls came to life.

DANCE

South of here the Stomp Dance fire lasts the night.
        Full-skirted women circle the grounds.
Their dresses swirl over turtle-shell shin rattles
        as men sing melodies older than words.

When I awaken in soft light the drum echoes
        in my ears with the swish of shells.
The day will be blessed. Where my feet touch Earth
        is a place of renewal. This day, I dance.

VI

—

TRAIL MARKER TREES

[We] cut the main-stem of a maple, just above the lowest branches, at a
growth stage when the [tip] would no longer regenerate. This resulted in
trees missing the upper dominant trunk, but with strong side branches
that resemble raised hands with open palms.

—TRAVERSE BAND OF ODAWA ELDERS

TRAIL MARKER TREE

Wisconsin

In Door County
my husband finds
a giant-limbed birch.

He offers tobacco
for those who lived
before us and left

this sign of aid
for travelers through
confusing roads.

My husband honors
Old Person Birch
and its relatives.

He breathes tobacco's
aromatic smoke,
our prayers.

TRAIL MARKER TREE

My Husband's Family History

Most of them have died but here
one stands on Lake Michigan's shore
between Egg Harbor and Sister Bay,
its enormous arms stretched open.
It waits for everyone to reach safety.

He tells me how to stake a sapling,
bend it askew, what his uncle taught
when he lived here. Maybe he climbed
this exact "Indian" trail marker tree,
a living archive, not folded pages.

Pliant young birch limbs bend
sideways to point trails in forests.
As the tree grows, the branch grows,
a luminous sign in snow or fog.
White bark gleams on darkest nights.

He pauses, looks away, travels years
back to his big family, Menominee,
a clan of summer migrant workers
in apple orchards, him a little boy.
This tree even then rose above floods.

AT DELAWARE RELATIVES' [STOLEN] VILLAGE IN OHIO

Abraham J. Baughman, a settler historian,
recalls the place where my Delaware relatives lived:

> *"A sycamore tree, which in the olden time*
> *cast its shade over the council house of the tribe,*
> *still stands like a monument from the past,*
> *grim and white, stretching its branches*
> *like skeleton arms in the attitude of benediction."*
>> [Does a "benediction" come to you from the sycamore?]

Baughman, a white settler, recalls my [stolen] homeland:

> *"A wild cherry tree stands several rods northeast,*
> *around which there was formerly a circular mound;*
> *but whether it was used as a circus ring for sports,*
> *or as a receptacle, is a matter of conjecture."*
>> [Do you wonder why no Lenape is left to ask?]

Baughman, who settled a [Lenape] town, recalls:

> *"The [Delaware] burial ground is at the west end*
> *of the knoll upon which Greentown was situated."*
>> [This burial place, to the West, should be avoided out of respect.]

Baughman, a town settler, who remembers, recalls from his memory:

> *"Heretofore, the ground has been held*
> *in superstitious [sic], if not sacred, veneration."*
>> [Baughman, do we both now venerate this sacred ground?]

NO FAIRY TALE

No ogres live in the Ohio forest,
          no wicked witches or stepmothers

dwell in hidden rock houses.
          The forest has no Garden of Eden.

Plants are gifts— food and medicine.
          Leaves spell an alphabet

sewn into clothing: strawberries
          for springtime and love.

Maple hands for sugar and bounty.
          Grape vines for sky's spirits.

Oak's strong wood is flesh
          for carved guardian Beings.

GRAPE

Midsummer grape vines
      climb cottonwoods trunks.
Their leaves are patchwork sails
      billowing sunward.

At Kansas powwow grounds
      grape-leaf designs edge shawls.
Men's garters glisten
      with grapevine beadwork.

There is a sacred alphabet:
      each plant a syllable sound.
Combinations of colors are prayers
      sewn into baskets, shirts, and belts.

After each leaf-fall a blue sky
      streams through the forest.
Gnarled vine scaffolds
      await next year's sun.

SETTLER ERASURE / DESUETUDE

*"It was the custom of Moravian Missionaries
to give to their camping-grounds names
the initials of which were carved on trees."*

In the name of the Moravian god they baptize / rename the trees.

*"In the course of time, the Susquehanna valleys
and New York forests were full of these mementos."*

They change "Susquehanna," Lenape for "River Oyster."
They baptize / rename each river as Christian.

"Localities were described in the itinerants' journals."

Moravian missionaries left initials and their Christian names for places.

"After the Pontiac Conspiracy this practice fell into desuetude."

"desuetude":

disuse   lapse

erasure   obsolescence   amnesia

abandonment   void   loss

obliteration   omission   dispossession

SEEDS

My bloodlines lead back
        to a day of murders
        to an oak-hickory forest—
        nearly erased from history yet

each word spoken since then
        is a seed of sound
        tended by grandparents
        each syllable a history.

Words bring Gnadenhutten to light—
        its sorrows and villains
        its heroes and saints
        its houses made from broken trees.

A tree cannot flee danger
        but its windblown seeds
        can endure fire
        can burst into life.

VII

UPSTREAM

On April 17, 1524, there were 15,000 Lenape people who met Giovanni de Verrazano on Manhattan. Seven major moves and 345 years later the last of the 985 survivors moved to Indian Territory, present day Oklahoma. That is a tough and resilient people.
—CHET BROOKS, CHIEF, DELAWARE TRIBE OF INDIANS, 2020

ACKNOWLEDGEMENT OF LENAPE LANDS

In Dawnland through five centuries
Lenapes fight:
Spanish, Swedes, Dutch,
        English, and United States settlers.

Blood-stained roads lead
away from New Jersey—
escape routes shared by Lenapes
        and runaway Africans.

Blood-memory stories mark
murders at Dutch Pavonia, at Coshocton,
at Gnadenhutten—where militia killed
        pacifist Lenape Christians.

Blood passes through mothers'
red wombs to landless children:
my mother, my grandfather,
        his parents and theirs.

Descendants live in Ramapough Mountains,
Appalachians of Pennsylvania and Ohio,
Canada, Wisconsin, Indiana, Missouri,
        Kansas, Oklahoma, Texas, Idaho:

Lenape people are alive,
hearts beating streams of red blood.

All the lands and waters where we continue,
        I acknowledge.

GEOGRAPHY LESSON

Diaspora

Some Lenape refugees settle upstream from the Little Muskingum River
    site of the Gnadenhutten massacre.

Some travel to Canada

Some return to mountains of New Jersey

Nowhere are they welcome.

My family is driven west to a Kansas farm
    until they are chased off by the Klan

        to Kansas City, Turtle Hill,
        always refugees.

MORE THAN PLACE NAMES

A Creek elder told me
      the valleys around Wooster are peopled with Delaware descendants.
A white elder told me
      the Lehigh area is peopled with Delaware descendants.
A Lenape elder told me
      we survive diseases, massacres, starvations, and swindlers.
My uncle told me
      I inherit this blood:

Killbuck's Creek named for a Lenape chief, 1764

Mohican Johnstown named for a chief of the Mohegans, John, on the west side of the Jeromefork

Beaver-Hat, south of Wooster, named for *Paupelenan*, an Indian chief and his residence *Chauquecake*, Apple Orchard

Jeromeville named for John Baptiste Jerome, where Captain Pipe and Lenape veterans of Fallen Timbers Battle settled

Katotawa where, on the banks of the Polk River, Katotawa (or Cha-tacht-a-waugh) "often pitched his tent and fished"

Journeycake, now Linwood in Kansas, named for Charles Journeycake or Neshepanah-cumin, born near the Upper Sandusky in Ohio and great-grandfather of my friend Janet Allen

CENSUS FORM

What Color I[ndian]?

Bair, Daniel – I[ndian] – Male – 61 – East Union Township

"Color": Choose one:

Whites, W	Blacks, B
Mulattos, Mu	Chinese, C
√ Indians, I	

> [Was it hot that day with swampy wet air,
> blackberries ripening along Apple Creek
> as the census taker arrived?]

Agriculture Schedule 2:

> [Was it hot that day,
> June fireflies at twilight,
> silty well water proffered
> as refreshment for the census taker?]

15 acres

Land including grass in rotation, pasture, woodland

3 acres

"Unimproved," "old fields"

> [Was it hot that June day with woodlands
> squirrels bickering? Goldfinches in mulberries?
> Did bears ramble through "unimproved" fields?
> Did the census taker color you "Indian"?]

OHIO

Footstones in a Family Cemetery

Near Apple Creek, four "footstones" for infants,
simple field stones, mark graves—granite,
not marble, just large enough to stop a plow.

The lost little ones blend with sod, their dust
entwined with grass and muck, still a presence
on the Bairs' farm now sold to the Stauffers.

White or Lenape or both—the families left
no other record but this overgrown acre.
Little relatives lie here, undiminished.

TRAILS OF MY RELATIVES

Ohio to Kansas

*

A forest trail runs to my twice-great-
grandparents' farm, their apple orchard,
a Lenape settlement on Sugar Creek
in Ohio, beyond the reach of militia.

When whites arrive my relatives
sell corn and apples, buy land deeds,
dress in fitted, sewn shirts at census time.
Mark graves with stones, not crosses.

*

In Kansas, bushwhackers rob
homesteads, shovel "live coals
from the fireplace onto mattresses,
setting fire to their cabins."

Veterans of the Indian Home Guard,
2nd Regiment-Delaware company,
return to more violence at home:
war on women, children, and elders.

The abolitionist governor arrives
from the Civil War and seizes
Lenape cornfields. He destroys
the Big House, a place of prayers.

The governor uses the scrap lumber
for a pigpen. Charred spars rise
over emptied Delaware lands.
He hopes no one will remember this theft.

*

Great-Grandfather plants apples
for cider, raises corn and hogs.
He avoids the tough railroad workers,
roughneck oilmen, and local cowboys.

Great-Grandmother carries a derringer
in her pocketbook. She always wears a coat
and never enters a church. On her gravestone
they etch a floral beadwork design. No cross.

MARY ANN (BAIR / BEAR / BARE)

Brown mica eyes with black
pinhole pupils focus on mine—
across a timespan.

In her portrait I see:

> Her black hair is pulled tight
> from her forehead and tilted ears.

The paper's edges are embossed stars
and twining vines reaching for the sky.

Killbuck Creek ran in her bloodstream,
then dull topaz of the Cottonwood in Kansas
where she died upriver from where

I was born twenty-five years later—

> our slow dance through
> the same water
> not quite touching.

The line of her mouth downturns.
She is a wordless woman speaking.

> Census takers changed her father's name
> from Bair to Bear to Bare.

Around her small face, I see a ruff of lace.
A necklace pendant gleams white—
> maybe bone, maybe pearl.

DESCENDANCY

Grandfather
    here is the space where I list Lenape stories you told

    _____

    here is the space where you chose to remain silent

    _____

    here is how many Indigenous stories you told me about:

        Romances of "Indian" lovers killing themselves: 0
        Movie parts of "Indian" extras falling off horses: 0
        Fake shamans: 0
        Per capita payments: 0

    here is what you told me to fight against:

        Corporate greed:
        No person is worth a million dollars.

        The Ku Klux Klan:
        They came in the torchlit night with tar and feathers.

        Union busters:
        *We wore paper bags over our heads with holes for eyes
        so they couldn't identify us and kill us.*

Grandfather, wanishi, thank you.

VIII

THE CONTINUOUSLY GIVING FOREST

Image Courtesy of Library Company of Philadelphia

The Moravian missionaries who came to the Lehigh Valley in the 1740s soon established several missions among the Delaware and Mahicans. This 1757 engraving shows Indians separated into male and female groups to receive baptism.
—EXPLORE PA HISTORY

BAPTISM OF MORAVIAN INDIAN CONVERTS, PENNSYLVANIA, 1757

*

The preacher pours water from a grail. A kneeling
  man, head bowed, learns his new
    Christian name.

Central in the chapel is the baptismal font,
  lit through three windows—
    a trinity.

Outside the panes one roofline tilts
  and hills recede under a forest
    canopy.

Two men wait, white cotton gowns
  covering their nakedness. Their hair
    is shorn.

*

For my baptism at twelve, I stood, no kneeling,
  silent as the minister traced
    a simple cross—

symbol of Earth in alchemy or, tilted, a chi / X,
  Greek letter, or in Lenape rock glyphs,
    a star.

Elm boughs arched over the church—green
  before Dutch elm disease turned
    them black.

What choice did I have, with death a certain destiny?
  Amidst griefs, this proffered moment
    of maybe.

THE FOREST

Roots

"When a root feels its way forward in the ground. . ."
        [footpath   pike   trail   course   trace]

"If the root encounters toxic substances. . . ."
        [nitrate dead zone   phosphorus   mire
                petroleum slick   sewage   bracken]

        [pestilence   massacre   ethnic cleansing
        factions   fractions   paper genocide]

"The root tip changes direction. . ."
        [detour   portage   fork   oxbow]

        [removal   relocation   reservation]

". . .danger steers the growing root."
        [seepage   spring   feeder   aquifer]

        [reconnection   wholeness   network]

THE FOREST

Warnings

Acacia trees send warnings to other trees
        acrid gases in the air.
They witness and send warnings to all of us.

Warnings of Jacob and Thomas, witnesses,
        save Lenapes of Shoenbrunn from death.
Jacob and Thomas see danger, send us a warning.

Josephine Ancie Plake's grandmother, a witness,
        saves Munsee hunters.
Josephine Ancie Plake sends us this warning.

THE FOREST

Damage

Burned-out forests
  Lightning-struck forests

Chopped and cleared forests
  Axed forests

Forests trampled and cannonballed
  Blighted forests

Charred-stump forests
  Old growth forests logged

Harvested forests
  Bulldozed and toppled forests

Strip-mined forests
  Forests replaced by food factories

"OHIO" MEANS "CONTINUOUSLY GIVING RIVER"

Ohio: "From '*ohi:yo*,' 'continuously giving river' in language of the Senecas."
[Great-uncle was named Ohio, the last child born before Kansas.]

Ohio: "Vast swamp forests of elm, ash, beech, pin oak, and maples."
[elm bark tea, beechnut meal, roasted acorns, maple sap]

Ohio: "To the east, a large cranberry bog covered by water."
[dried cranberries for winter, boiled with geese, ducks, trout, bass]

Ohio: "Hunting camps on the headwaters."
[bears, deer, forest buffalo, rabbits, squirrels, raccoons, beaver]

Ohio: "Wetlands produced abundant game even after most sections of the country were farmed."
[the "unimproved" lands of my grandparents in Ohio]

IX

—

FIRE TRAILS

In the same night of the massacre the white men set fire to all the houses of Gnaden-
hutten, and to the slaughterhouses among the rest. The dead bodies were but partially
consumed, and their bones remained to bleach in the sun until after some twenty
years they received interment by friendly hands. By the light of the burning village
the murderers then departed, rending the air with shouts and yells more savage than
ever arose in the wilderness before, carrying with them the scalps, about fifty horses,
numerous blankets, and some other articles of plunder, which they exposed to public
sale in Pittsburgh.

—GNADENHUTTEN MONUMENT SOCIETY, 1870

ARCHAEOLOGICAL REPORT I

Fire

Shoenbrunn / Beautiful Spring in Ohio, 3000 years old:
      where archeologists find

    chipped flint tools   and the debris—   what survives flames.

Pennsylvania, 1781: No artifact remains of Moravian forced removal
      yet archeologists find at their village:

        "the most striking   widespread   presence of   hearths"—

           fire-cracked rock underlying embers

           for   cooking   processing tools   warmth—

           stone the only witness of their prayers.

ARCHAEOLOGICAL REPORT II

Corrections

Archaeologists *"save"* [convert to data]
a significant Delaware site

> in Pennsylvania / Lenapehoking
> [Jacob's] Plains Township

on the Susquehanna, originally occupied by
> a Delaware [Unami] Chief
> Jacob [Teedyuscung].

Prior to the Revolutionary War
> many individuals
> farmed along the river
> [corn, beans, squash, orchards]
> raised livestock
> [cattle, hogs, poultry, rabbits].

Jacob [Teedyuscung] died
> as a result of his house being burned
>> [by the colonists].

The surviving Delawares [Unami] fled
> [except for those, undocumented, who stayed behind].

FIRE TERROR / FIRE ERASURE

Barn burning:
another weapon
colonists use as
slash-and-burn
thievery
from the Atlantic
to western deserts.

> *"Chief Armstrong*
> *was assured*
> *Greentown's*
> *Delaware-owned*
> *property would be*
> *inventoried*
> *and protected*
> *until peace ensued."*

Can you see
the smoke shrouds?
Smell the stench?
Find fire-blackened
arrowheads
turned up in fields
after every rain?

> *"The same day*
> *a faction*
> *of militia men*
> *who 'assisted'*
> *in removal*
> *stayed behind,*
> *plundered,*
> *and set fire."*

FAMILY RESEARCH

Three Brothers

Polished granite gravestones catch sunrise fire
      each morning in Flint Hills air purified by wind.
           Engraved names are Charles, Harry, and Frank.

During the nineteen-aughts, my mother told me,
        Charlie inherited the bank
        Harry the farm
        Her father Frank went to pharmacy school.

        [She never knew the Klan
        drove her grandparents from the farm
        with burning torches.]

        [She never knew she got it wrong.]

City directories and census records show:

    Charles
        bought the bank from Samuel Cobb,
            Native grandfather of Nancy Landon Kassebaum.

    Harry
        repurchased the family homestead in 1929
            just before the Stock Market Crash.
        He raised wheat and hunted.

    Frank the youngest, my mother's father,
        worked as a stenographer
        rode the rails
        picked apples in Oregon
        clerked in Kansas drug stores
        worked the docks of Oakland
        raised rabbits for county fair prize money
        switched train cars in a Kansas roundhouse
        drove a taxi
        buried two children
        raised two children
        a girl and a boy.

Uncle Harry I met once, at your funeral, Grandfather. He was a haunted, hollow-eyed man who nodded at me before turning into this memory.

In a family photograph after the funeral, I am an afterthought in the back row. There is my mother in front with her cousins and in the center Uncle Harry, his eyes small stars in the black-and-white print.

I report something like what really happened that afternoon, as the sun washed us in bright afternoon rays broken by deep shadows.

JANE'S MAZE, DELAWARE "HALF-BREED TRACT"

I go North on White Clay Road past the river's
        broken ice and bald eagles fishing

into the floodplain with staggered Ice Age
        terraces distant ahead of me,

East on Wellman Road and jagged turns,
        dips through rounded hills

to the T intersection gravel road to Dabinawa,
        turning right into the dead end.

Trees outline an entrance, a statue—Celtic
        and Algonquin, Jane's bloodlines.

Her body is a maze of old and new worlds:
        black hair, black eyes, red blood.

Cedar grows to the North, fire burns to the South.
        Fallen trees shape a rough outer fence.

I circle my way to stations of the four-way cross,
        a medicine wheel to enter from the East.

X

—

OHIO

Memorials

Monument in Memory of the Gnadenhutten Martyrs, who were
Massacred by the Indians, Nov. 24, 1755—Lehighton, Pa.
Published by J. G. Rauch, Slatington, Pa.

I am descended from and a current member of the Delaware Nation at Moravian-town. My great-great-grandfather Christian Moses Stonefish came back to Gnaden-hutten 90 years after the massacre to dedicate that stone obelisk commemorating the event. I agree with you about the heaviness in the air, it is palpable.

—GERARD F. HEATH, MARCH 14, 2017

GNADENHUTTEN MEMORIAL DEDICATION, 1872

The Moravian brethren met at Gnadenhutten
        ninety years after. With ceremonies

they dedicated a carved stone monument
        to the memory of Delaware converts who perished

"in triumph" at the old Mission Church.
        Four Moravian Delawares removed the drape.

One was Christian Moses Stonefish—
the great-grandson of Joseph Shabosh,

the first Lenape victim of the marauders
        at Gnadenhutten, Ohio, 1782.

MEMORIAL

The Cost

Admission to the Gnadenhutten Monument & Museum is free.
    "This is the oldest settlement in Ohio."
Admission to the Gnadenhutten Monument & Museum is free.
    "Established in 1772 by a Mohican elder and Christian Indians."
Admission to the Gnadenhutten Monument & Museum is free.
    "In 1782 nearly 100 of the Indian residents were killed."
Admission to the Gnadenhutten Monument & Museum is free.
    "A 35-foot memorial recognizes those killed in the massacre."
Admission to the Gnadenhutten Monument & Museum is free.
    "A museum displays artifacts and an arrowhead collection."
Admission to the Gnadenhutten Monument & Museum is free.
    "There is also a reconstructed church."
Admission to the Gnadenhutten Monument & Museum is free.

POSTCARD

"The Monument, Gnadenhutten, Ohio"

> To: Miss Kate Adams Canton Ohio 1107 S. Market St.
> Postmark: July 20, 1907, GNAD OHIO

THE MONUMENT, GNADENHUTTEN, OHIO.
Inscribed: Here Triumphed in Death Ninety Christian Indians, March 8, 1782.

"Here Triumphed in Death 90 Christian Indians, March 8, 1782."

"'Having a fine time.' B.D.H."

[Dear B.D.H.,
What is a "fine time" in a cemetery of scalped children and adults?
What is a "fine time" in a cemetery of pacifist victims?
What is a "fine time" in a cemetery of 96 murdered people?
What is a "fine time" in a cemetery of genocide conquest?]

[Dear B.D.H.,
What is a bad time?]

SIGNAGE

"Burial Site of Indian Martyrs"

Not an archaeological "burial mound" like a midden of mussel shells
Not a cathedral site with crosses and votive candles for sale

Not a site looted by pot hunters digging for free artifacts
Not a saint's chapel with stained glass windows

Not an "Indian" mound plowed over in fields
Not a history book with facts of a massacre

Not a living community of people
Not a memorial to peace

Not an apology
Not a restitution

"THE WHITE MEN CALLED THEM TO RETURN"

A Transcription

A Munsee (Delaware) account of Knāngihitinany (Gnadenhutten)

Josephine Ancie Plake, Munsee resident of Kansas, 1912, tells the recorder from the Smithsonian Institute:

Whites crowded the Munsees out of Pennsylvania, so they went to Gnadenhutten, Ohio.

They lived there for quite some time with their preacher. They had good fields, many cattle, and hogs.

When the [Revolutionary] War came, the British forced them to leave their prosperous lands and move to a [prison] camp on the Sandusky River.

The Munsees and the Moravian preacher stayed there all winter because of the war.

Then the white men from Pennsylvania called for them to return [to their Ohio homes], to renew their friendship.

The Munsees, they did go back again to collect field corn, but their preacher, an old man, stayed behind with some others.

When the Munsees got to Gnadenhutten, their white friends told them to wait in the church building. They said, "Stay, then we'll meet you there. We will fix our friendship."

The Munsees went into the church, almost a hundred of them.

While they waited, they prayed and sang hymns.

Then as the Moravians waited in the church, a woman's child cried. She took it outdoors.

She looked up the road and saw a group of whites on horseback riding toward her. She saw they had sabers of war.

She hid in the brush with her child.

She watched while the whites surrounded the church. Then they entered and commenced killing all the Indians.

Blood began to pour [from between the church house's boards].

Then the whites came outside and set the church on fire.

Ninety-six people died.

When the Munsee woman saw this, she fled.

She went to find a hunting party of Munsees [who had not gone into the church with everyone else].

The woman walked three days with her child until she found the hunters.

They went back to Gnadenhutten to look for survivors. [There were none].

Then they fled to Canada.

"THE WHITE MEN CALLED THEM TO RETURN"

An Interrogation

In the story, a Munsee woman tells about the whites "calling" them to return to Gnadenhutten.

> Did the whites plan the massacre from the beginning?
> What was that "calling"? A written message? A messenger?

The woman and her child found Munsee hunters three days later.

> What did they eat? Where did they sleep?
> Did the hunters leave glyph markings on trees?

What grief did the woman and her child carry in their bodies after seeing the burned, scalped corpses?

How many generations does that grief last? Did the granddaughter Josephine Ancie Plake also know that grief in her body?

Do grandchildren dream their ancestors' nightmares?

What prayers sustained them? Can sustain us?

A GAMBLER'S ODDS

My Lenape grandfather pulls out a deck of cards and deals.
      I'm nine. We sit at a table under the window.

He lives in rented rooms above the liquor store.
      Now I see this scene from the outside looking in,

slow motion, as we play gin rummy and silently count cards.
      I win a few times but mostly lose. So I learn how

to hold my temper. Patience. Respect for his experience.
      My grandfather reshuffles the cards. Try again.

When I cut, he teaches spells: "Cut 'em thin, bound to win."
      The next time, "Cut 'em thick, beat 'em quick."

He tells how he escaped the union busters, how sometimes
      he lost but always he fought on, even at risk of death.

He does not talk about his twins, one a stillbirth, the other
      sickly all her short life, or how he had a good job

but lost it gambling. He never had a winning streak yet here
      he is teaching a shy child how to fight, how to take chances.

STOMP DANCE, WYANDOTTE COUNTY, KANSAS

The lead man lifts his black hat and calls from the center.

I wait for the tail-end of the man-woman procession. Lead women are shell shakers. Double-time steps rustle turtle-shell rattles tied to shins.

Men sing and sing loud. Women step-step hard. The inner circle turns sideways to the fire.

My grandfather and grandmother lived on Lenape land near this spot. Their footprints remain in this ground.

The leader raises his arm for each new song. Men answer. Their breath lifts into wind.

I remember Jo sa yi, what he said about Tobacco. The head man offers it to fire.

I remember the Fall Leaf family and their stomp ground near Copan. I remember Cherokees who dance, Redbird Smith's descendants Croslin and Benny.

She-shush of shells mixes with songs older than the mounds.

We dance.

ACKNOWLEDGMENTS

The author is grateful to the editors of these previous publications:

"Before the Gnadenhutten Massacre" and "Trail Marker Tree" in *Apogee Journal*, online "Place[meant]" series, 18 March, 2018; reprinted in *Shadow Light* (Red Mountain Press)

"A Land Acknowledgement," *The Poetry Co-op*, Aug. 8, 2022, online, *150kansaspoems.wordpress.com*

"Northwest Territory, on the Ohio, 1790," *Indigenous Nations Poets Instagram*, Aug. 12, 2022

"Walking with My Delaware Grandfather, *Poetry Foundation*, 2014; reprinted in *On Being Project*, April 2022; reprinted in *Poetry of Presence: An Anthology of Mindfulness Poems*, Volume 2 (Grayson Books)

"Wyandotte County Stomp Dance," *Level Land: Poems for and About the I35 Corridor*, eds. Todd Fuller and Crag Hill (Lamar University Press), reprint; *Shadow Light* (Red Mountain Press)

Many supporters helped with this project, especially early readers, including Melissa Carr, Caryn Mirriam-Goldberg, Joe Harrington, and Linda Rodriguez. All generations of my family are always with me. My late husband Thomas Pecore Weso encouraged me to write this difficult book situated on the margins. His spirit lives on.

Gratitude to Elizabeth Wilder of the University of Arizona Press, who believed in this project and offered kind counsel throughout, and to Amanda Krause for her expert guidance through the editorial, design, and production phases. I further appreciate the enthusiasm of Abby Mogollon, Mary Reynolds, and Cameron Louie, who are the marketing team. The beautiful cover is from the painting *On Lenape Land* by Susan Hoenig, and Leigh McDonald, art director, worked to get the perfect integration of cover and interior with content. Thank you also to Sara Thaxton, who created the ebook.

Much appreciation to Sun Tracks series editor Ofelia Zepeda, who dedicates her life to good words and the books that hold some of them.

NOTES

The name "Delaware" is a term European colonists used for Lenape peoples, because of their proximity to the Delaware River. The term "Lenape" in the Algonkian language includes all people of this heritage. Munsee is a subtribe of Lenape with a distinct dialect. Various other Algonkian-speaking refugees were in the congregation of Gnadenhutten.

Section I: "Their Names: First Shots at Gnadenhutten, 1782" uses texts from Edmund De Schweinitz, author of Moravian missionary David Zeisberger's biography, *The Life and Times of David Zeisberger*. Many quotations and accounts of the Gnadenhutten massacre and name lists come from this 1871 source, especially chapters 35–37. De Schweinitz uses Ziesberger's journal; John Heckewelder's writings; Doddridge's *Notes, Pennsylvania Archives*, vol. ix; and Taylor's *History of Ohio*. The language of these sources—its extravagances and circumlocutions—informs my own diction. "Weapon of Choice, the Gnadenhutten Massacre, 1782" references online dictionaries, "Tomahawk History," and "A Note on Scalp Bounties in Pennsylvania" by Henry J. Young. Young's article on scalp bounties provides facts for "Genocide Mathematics" in Section II. "A Mixed-Blood's Questions" is inspired by Linda Hogan's poem in *Seeing Through the Sun*, "In my left pocket a Chickasaw hand / rests on the bone of the pelvis. / In my right pocket / a white hand. Don't worry. It's mine."

Section II: "Big Miller the Indian Fighter: A Conversation with a Timeline" uses sources from the website *Pennsylvania.Archives*, Battalion report, Williston, Draper Papers.

Section III: The opening quotation is from *True History of the Massacre*, attributed to the Gnadenhutten Monument Society, 1870. Among sources for "A Delaware Catechism" is "Historic American Indian Tribes of Ohio." "Colonial Belief" uses a discussion of Canaanites as equivalent to Indigenous Americans in Thomas Slaughter's *The Whiskey Rebellion* and William Farrar's "The Moravian Massacre." The quotation is from Farrar.

Section IV: Texts of the Lord's Prayer are in William Heller, and I quote Heller in "Hymns in the Forest" (p. 103).

Section V: William Dean Howell's quotation is from *Three Villages.* "High-Ways" uses quotations from the Ohio Historical Society's web publication *Historic American Indian Tribes of Ohio*, pp. 3-4. "Geography Lesson: Of Rivers and Mountains and Stars" quotes Heller, from "The Aborigines." The term "Lenapehoking" means Lenape, or Delaware, homeland.

Section VI: The first two poems refer to a tree, illustrated on a previous page, on the grounds of Write On Door County in Juddville, Wisconsin. Gratitude to WODC and Jared Santek for residencies at that site. An article by William McClain informs this section. "Settler Erasure / Desuetude" refers to De Schweinitz, pp. 122–23. "Seeds" refers to ideas in Peter Wolleben's *The Hidden Life of Trees*, p. 186.

Section VII: Historic sources for the geographic names of Ohio in this section's poems include A. J. Baughman's *A History of the Pioneer and Modern Times of Ashland County, Ohio* (pp. 185–86 and p. 78) and S. H. Mitchell's *The Indian Chief, Journeycake*, p. 20. "Trails of My Relatives: Ohio to Kansas" quotes "Warriors for the Union" by Deborah Nichols and Laurence M. Hauptman, and Michael Caron told me about destruction of the Big House, based on his research.

Section VIII: "The Forest: Roots" quotes Peter Wohlleben, p. 183; "The Forest: Warnings" refers to information from Wohlleben, p. 7 ("The acacia . . ."). "Ohio: Continuously Giving River" refers to Lucille Lang Day's poem "Names of the States," a broadside, used with permission.

Section IX: In "Archaeological Report II: Corrections," Susan Bachor, Eastern Representative, Delaware Tribe, reports on the Jacob Plains site. "Fire Terror / Fire Erasure" quotes an Ohio highway marker in Ashland County, online, *Historicalmarkerproject.com.*

Section X: Gerard F. Heath's opening quotation is from the *History in Stone* blog, the comments section, reprinted on the site of the Gnadenhutten Historical Museum. The first poem quotes from the Gnadenhutten Monument Society publication. The vintage postcards in this section come from eBay. "Memorial: The Cost" quotes the website Gnadenhutten Museum & Historical Park | Ohio Traveler, accessed Nov. 7, 2023. I am indebted to Michael Ford for calling my attention to the Smithsonian transcription of Josephine Ancie Plake's oral account from the Munsee community who reside in the Ottawa, Kansas, area of Chippewa Hills. He has made this available in printed form, *Munsee Transcription Smithsonian Ethnologist Truman Michaelson 1912–1913*, available on Kindle. For "Stomp Dance, Kansas" and other poems, my gratitude to Kansas Delaware tribal members Linda Webb Graff, Kameran Zeigler, Carol Rowe, Kenny Vernoy, and Jim Grinter. Further appreciation to Janet Allen and Joshua Falleaf.

SOURCES

Bachor, Susan. "Historic Delaware Site Saved in Pennsylvania." *Delaware Indian News* / Lënapeí Pampil 39, no. 3 (July 2016): 9. https://delawaretribe.org/wp-content/uploads/din-2016-07.pdf.

Baughman, Abraham J. *History of Ashland County*. Vol.1. Chicago: S.J. Clarke Publishing Co., 1909. https://www.google.com/books/edition/History_of_Ashland_County_Ohio/R9UyAQAAMAAJ?hl=en.

Brooks, Chet. "From the Desk of Chief Chet Brooks." *Delaware Indian News* 43, no. 2 (July 2020).

Bull, James H. *The Bulls of Parkeomink, Montgomery County, Pennsylvania, and Their Descendants*. Historical Society of Norristown, Pa., June 1, 1907.

De Schweinitz, Edmund. *The Life and Times of David Zeisberger: The Western Pioneer and Apostle*. 1870. https://www.google.com/books/edition/The_Life_and_Times_of_David_Zeisberger/xtX2QrNmmiUC?hl=en&gbpv=1.

Day, Lucille Lang. "Names of the States." In *Birds of San Pancho*. Blue Light Press, 2020.

Farrar, William M. "The Moravian Massacre." *Ohio Archeological and History Society Publications* 3. Paper presented at the Sixth Annual Meeting of the Ohio History Society at Columbus, February 1891. https://resources.ohiohistory.org/ohj/search/display.php?page=6&ipp=20&searchterm=Array&vol=3&pages=261-315.

Franklin, Benjamin. Benjamin Franklin to James Hutton, July 7, 1782, *Founders Online*. https://founders.archives.gov/documents/Franklin/01-37-02-0377.

Gnadenhutten Monument Society. *True History of the Massacre of Ninety-six Christian Indians at Gnadenhutten, Ohio, March 8th, 1782*. New Philadelphia, Ohio: Gnadenhutten Monument Society, 1870. https://archive.org/details/truehistoryofmas00lcgnad.

"Gnadenhutten Museum." *Trip Advisor*. https://www.tripadvisor.com/Attraction_Review-g50383-d4809795-Reviews-Gnadenhutten_Museum-Gnadenhutten_Ohio.html.

Heath, Gerard F. "The Massacre at Gnadenhutten," comment, History in Stone, *Blogspot.com*, March 14, 2017. https://historyinstone.blogspot.com/2014/10/massacre-at-gnadenhutten.html.

Heller, William J. *History of Northampton County and the Grand Valley of the Lehigh* 1. Boston: The American Historical Society, 1920.

"Historic American Indian Tribes of Ohio." *Ohio Historical Society*. https://www.rrcs.org/downloads/ohios%20historic%20indians%2038%20pages.pdf.

History in Stone (blog). "The Massacre at Gnadenhutten," *Blogspot.com*, Oct. 6, 2014. https://historyinstone.blogspot.com/2014/10/massacre-at-gnadenhutten.html

Hogan, Linda. *Seeing Through the Sun*. Amherst: University of Massachusetts Press, 1985.

Holmes, Col. J.T. *The American Family of Reverend Obadiah Holmes*. Columbus, Ohio: 1915.

Howells, William Dean. "Gnadenhutten." *Three Villages*. Boston: James R. Osgood and Co., 1884. https://en
.wikisource.org/wiki/Three_Villages.

Keener, Deborah. "Small Family Cemetery Endangered." *Wayne Ancestors* 11, no. 2 (April/March 2001): 1+.

Mitchell, S. H. *The Indian Chief, Journeycake*. Philadelphia, Pa.: American Baptist Publication Society, 1895.
https://archive.org/details/indianchiefoomitcrich.

McClain, William. "Mysteries of the Trail-Marker Trees." *The Illinois Steward, University of Illinois Extension*.
Cited in https://ottawarewind.com/2016/08/07/strange-things-old-native-trails-once-marked-by-bent
-trees/.

McClain, William. "Oaks as Native American Trail Marker Tree." *International Oak Journal* 17 (Spring 2006):
45-48. https://www.internationaloaksociety.org/sites/default/files/files/IO/IOS%20Journal%20%2317/
International%20Oaks%20No.%2017%20-%20Oaks%20as%20Native%20American%20Trail%20Marker
%20Trees%20-%20William%20McClain.pdf.

Nichols, Deborah and Laurence M. Hauptman "Warriors for the Union." *Civil War Times* (1996). https://
delawaretribe.org/wp-content/uploads/warriors.pdf

Perry, Lynette and Manny Skolnick. *Keeper of the Delaware Dolls*. Lincoln: University of Nebraska Press, 1999.

Plake, Josephine Acie. "Ethnographic and Linguistic Field Notes from the Munsee in Kansas and Delaware in
Oklahoma." Oral story recorded by Truman Michelson, National Museum of Natural History, National
Anthropological Archives. Online Smithsonian Institute. Si.edu. https://edan.si.edu/slideshow/viewer/
?eadrefid=NAA.MS2776

Powhatan, Rose. "Surviving Document Genocide," in *The People Who Stayed: Southeastern Indian Writing after
Removal*, edited by Geary Hobson, Janet McAdams, and Kathryn Walkiewic. University of Oklahoma
Press, 2012.

Slaughter, Thomas P. *The Whiskey Rebellion*. New York: Oxford University Press, 1988.

Sterner, Eric. "Moravians in the Middle: The Gnadenhutten Massacre." *Journal of the American Revolution*. Feb.
6, 2018. https://allthingsliberty.com/2018/02/moravians-middle-gnadenhutten-massacre/.

"Tomahawk History." 2014. http://www.hawkthrowing.com/history-of-tomahawks.html.

Traverse Band of Odawa elders. Quoted by Ladislav Hanka in "Land of the Crooked Tree, L'Arbre Croche,
Waganakising." *Dreams of a Wandering Naturalist: Books and Prints of Ladislav Hanka*. https://www
.ladislavhanka.com/HankaSobota_Traveling_Book_Show/Crooked_Trees.html.

Williston, George C. "The 1782 Volunteer Militia from Washington County, Pa. and their Moravian Indian
Victims." http://freepages.genealogy.rootsweb.ancestry.com/~gwilli824/moravian.html.

Wohlleben, Peter. *The Hidden Life of Trees*. Vancouver: Greystone Books, 2015.

Young, Henry J. "A Note on Scalp Bounties in Pennsylvania." *Pennsylvania History*, 1957. https://journals.psu
.edu/phj/article/view/22543/22312.

ILLUSTRATIONS

Section I: Illustration from Henry Howe's 1852 book *Historical Collections of the Great West*, published in Cincinnati. Wikipedia.

Section III: *Zeisberger Preaching to the Indians* is an engraving after an 1862 painting by Christian Schussele, based on Edmund De Schweinitz's biography. The event was Zeisberger's first sermon to Indigenous people, Senecas. Library of Congress, no known restrictions on image.

Section IV: Gnadenhutten spelling book, title page of David Zeisberger's *Essay of a Delaware-Indian and English Spelling-Book*, published in 1776, is available at *Archive.org* and *openlibrary.org*.

Section V: Illustration courtesy of the Ohio History Connection, SA1039AV-B14F01-005-001, Ohio Memory at https://ohiomemory.ohiohistory.org/archives/2686.

Section VI: Trail Marker Tree photograph by Denise Low, at Write On Door County writing center in Juddville, Wisconsin.

Section VII: Photograph of Mary Ann Bair is in the author's personal collection.

Section VIII: "Engraving of Baptism of Indian converts in Bethlehem, Pennsylvania, 1757," *Explore Pennsylvania History*, online photograph Courtesy of The Library Company of Philadelphia, https://librarycompany.org/using-the-library/rightsrepro/#/.

Section X: Vintage postcards are in the author's personal collection. The "Burial Site of Indian Martyrs" photograph is from Wikipedia.

ABOUT THE AUTHOR

Denise Low, former Kansas Poet Laureate, is a founding board member of Indigenous Nations Poets. Her books include *Shadow Light: Poems, The Turtle's Beating Heart: One Family's Story of Lenape Survival,* and *A Casino Bestiary.* Her *Northern Cheyenne Ledger Art by Fort Robinson Breakout Survivors* won a Kansas Notable Book Award. She founded the creative writing program at Haskell Indian Nations University and is a past board president of the Associated Writers and Writing Programs. She currently is a literary co-director for The 222 in Sonoma County, California, and on the advisory board of Write On Door County. Low has Northern European and Lenape (Delaware) heritage. www.deniselow.net.